THE BITCOIN GUIDE

SIMPLE STEP BY STEP

THE BEGINNERS GUIDE TO EASILY BUY, INVEST, SECURED AND TRADE WITH BITCOIN AND OTHER CRYPTOCURRENCY PLATFORM

MARK THOMAS

Copyright© 2020 Mark Thomas

All Right Reserved

CHAPTER ONE

INTRODUCTION
Why Bitcoin is Gaining Traction

CHAPTER TWO

What makes bitcoins important?
Bitcoins Are Scarce

CHAPTER THREE

Bitcoins Are Useful
Bitcoin has a Advantangeous Connection to the Market
Bitcoin's Price
Would You Be Able To Get Bitcoin For Free
Would I Be Able To Still Get Rich With Bitcoin?
When Is The Ideal Time To Purchase Bitcoin

OUR BITCOIN VALUE GRAPH

CHAPTER FOUR

Process To Invest In Bitcoins And Where To Buy
Record Nano X
TREZOR

Would It Be A Good Idea For You To Invest In Bitcoin Mining?
Keeping Away From Bitcoin Scams

CHAPTER FIVE

How Might I Avoid Bitcoin Scams?
What Is A Leave Trick?
Would I Be Able To Get My Cashback?
What Do I Do If I Feel I've Been Contacted By A Bitcoin Scammer?

CHAPTER SIX

FAQ
Is It Worth Investing In Bitcoin?
Are There Bitcoin Investment Plans?

CHAPTER ONE

INTRODUCTION

Considering putting resources into Bitcoin?

This book will lay out a few things you NEED to know before you purchase.

We will clarify:

- The essentials of putting resources into bitcoin
- Why it should be focused on
- How to purchase bitcoins

- How to ensure and appropriately secure your bitcoin in the event that you do choose to contribute

Why Bitcoin is Gaining Traction

The world is getting consistently reliant on the web.

So it's nothing unexpected that Bitcoin, safe, worldwide, and computerized cash has asserted the premium of financial specialists.

Bitcoin is borderless and worldwide

Bitcoin is available to everybody and gives an energizing occasion to dig into a completely new resource class.

Putting resources into bitcoin may appear to be frightening, however, realize that it requires some investment and exertion to see how Bitcoin functions.

Additionally, remember that the administrative points of view on Bitcoin worldwide are shifted. Recall that, and do your own assessment subject to where you live.

Why Invest in Bitcoin?

It appears senseless to certain individuals that one bitcoin can be worth a huge number of U.S. dollars.

CHAPTER TWO

What makes bitcoins important?

Bitcoins Are Scarce

We should look to gold as illustration cash. There is a limited proportion of gold on earth.

As new gold is mined, there is in every case less and less gold left and it gets more diligently and more costly to discover and mine.

A view from inside a drained gold mine

Consequently, alongside Gold's millennia-long history as a mechanism of trade, it has for some time been viewed as support against financial expansion.

Gold is an under-claimed resource, despite the fact that gold has gotten substantially more mainstream. In the event that you ask any national bank, any sovereign abundance store, any individual what level of their portfolio is in gold..., you'll see it to be very little... It's...imprudently small..., particularly when we're losing a money framework.

Beam Dalio, Legendary Hedge Fund Manager

The equivalent is valid with Bitcoin.

There may be 21 million Bitcoins, and as time goes on, they become progressively difficult to mine.

Examine Bitcoin's expanding rate and supply rate:

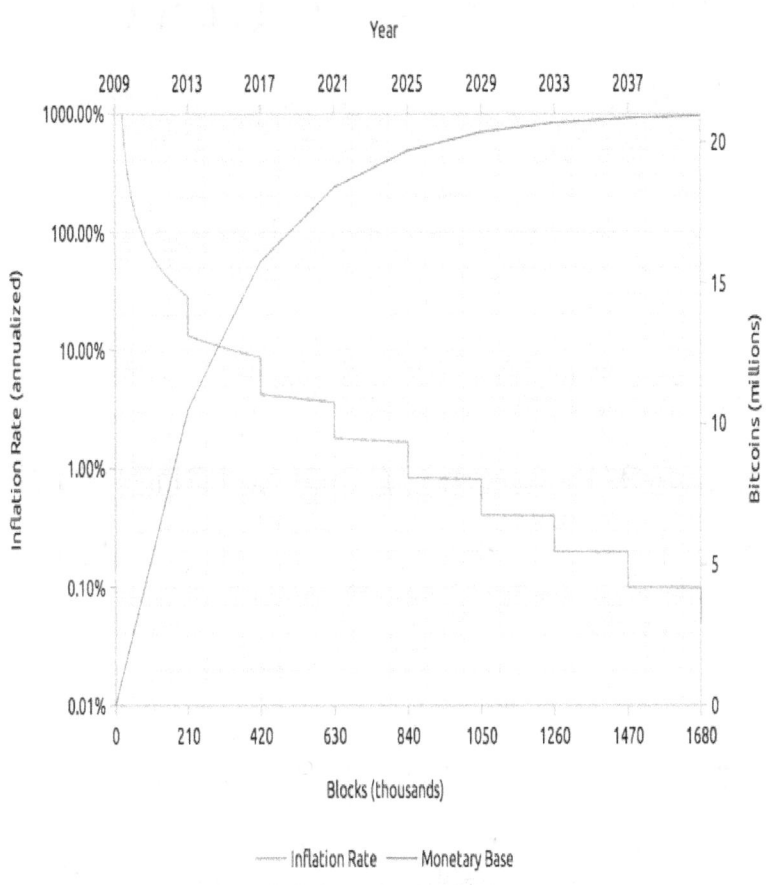

CHAPTER THREE
Bitcoins Are Useful

Notwithstanding being scant, bitcoins are helpful advanced resources.

Bitcoin gives sound and unsurprising financial arrangements that can be confirmed by anybody.

Bitcoin's financial approach is one of its most significant highlights. It's conceivable to see when new bitcoins are made when Bitcoin exchanges are made, or the number of bitcoins is available for use.

Bitbonkers.com is a great way to see the blockchain continuously

Bitcoins can be sent from anyplace on the planet to elsewhere on the planet. No bank can impede installments or close your record. Bitcoin is restriction safe cash.

Bitcoin's blockchain innovation and public record make cross fringe installments conceivable and furthermore gives a simple method to individuals to get away from bombed government financial arrangements.

The extension rate in Venezuela completed out at 10 million percent.

The web made information worldwide and easy to get to. A sound, worldwide money like Bitcoin will have a similar effect on the account and the worldwide economy.

On the off chance that you comprehend the expected effect of Bitcoin, it won't be difficult to comprehend why putting resources into bitcoin might be a smart thought.

Bitcoin has a Advantangeous Connection to the Market

Bitcoin is viewed as an uncorrelated resource, implying that there gives off an impression of being no connection between the exhibition of the customary stock and security markets and that of Bitcoin. This is attractive for dealers hoping to enhance hazard out of their portfolio. By adding Bitcoin to their portfolio, they can diminish the probability of a significant decline in stocks from unfavorably influencing their total assets.

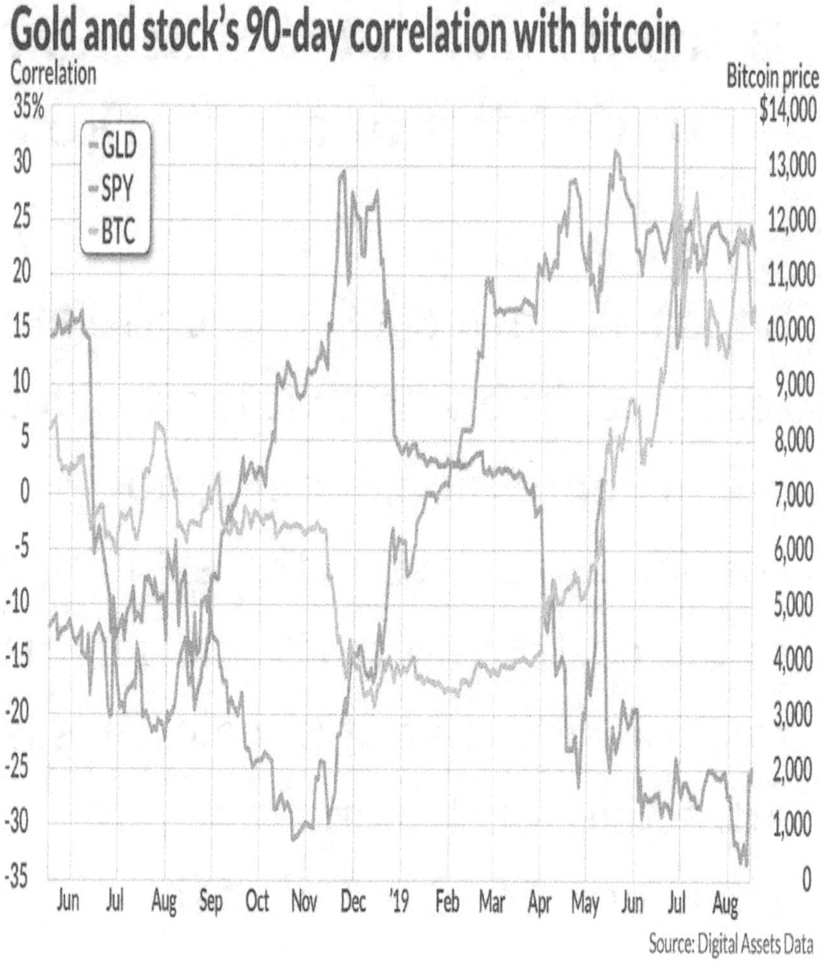

Gold and stock's 90-day correlation with bitcoin
Correlation
Bitcoin price
35%
30
25
20
15
10
5
0
-5
-10
-15
-20
-25
-30
-35
$14,000
13,000
12,000
11,000
10,000
9,000
8,000
7,000
6,000
5,000
4,000
3,000
2,000
1,000
0
GLD
SPY
BTC
Jun
Jul
Aug
Sep
Oct
Nov
Dec
'19
Feb
Mar
Apr
May
Jun
Jul
Aug
Source: Digital Assets Data

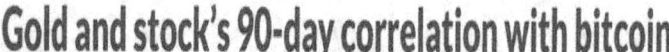

Bitcoin's Price

There is no official Bitcoin cost. Bitcoin's expense is set by whatever people are glad to pay.

Purchase Bitcoin Worldwide is a decent asset at the current and authentic cost.

Bitcoin's cost is for the most part appeared as the expense of one bitcoin. Notwithstanding, a digital currency trade will allow you to purchase any sum, and you can purchase short of what one bitcoin.

The following is a graph demonstrating Bitcoin's whole value history:

Would You Be Able To Get Bitcoin For Free

Bitcoin is cash. Individuals generally don't part with cash for nothing, so you should be exceptionally suspicious of anybody promising to give you Bitcoins free of charge. Be that as it may, you can here and there get modest quantities of Bitcoin with the expectation of complimentary when different trades and Bitcoin interest accounts offer you Bitcoin to open a record on their foundation. Contingent upon how much cash you reserve the records with, these offers range from about $10 to $250 worth of Bitcoin.

Block is presenting $250 in Bitcoin rewards when you open a record.

Would I Be Able To Still Get Rich With Bitcoin?

Nobody knows, and honestly, nobody will actually know. Any individual who vows to make you rich with Bitcoin is likely misleading you.

Bitcoin is as yet considered by most to be a dangerous venture and you ought to never contribute beyond what you can bear to lose. That being stated, exceptionally unstable resources will in general have the more noteworthy potential for return (coordinated by its potential for unbelievable misfortune). You ought to consistently counsel an authorized monetary organizer.

When Is The Ideal Time To Purchase Bitcoin

In like manner, with any market, nothing is unquestionable.

Anybody's speculation is just probably in the same class as anybody's with regards to foreseeing close to term Bitcoin costs.

Since its commencement, Bitcoin has commonly expanded in an incentive at an exceptionally high speed, trailed by a moderate, consistent ruin until it balances out.

Use devices like our Bitcoin value diagram to break down outlines and comprehend Bitcoin's value history.

Our Bitcoin value graph

Bitcoin is worldwide and consequently less influenced by any single nation's monetary circumstance or steadiness, fortunate or unfortunate.

For instance, a theory about the Chinese Yuan depreciating has, previously, caused more interest from China, which likewise pulled up the conversion scale on the U.S. also, Europe based trades.

We've additionally observed positively trending markets in Bitcoin in the United States bring about huge exchange occasions in business sectors with significantly less liquidity because of capital controls, for example, Korea. Because of Korea, these were known as the 'Kimchi Premium'

As an Experts note in Trading and Arbitrage in Cryptocurrency Markets,

The day by day normal value proportion between the US and

Korea between December 2017 to February 2018 arrived at 40% for a few days...We gauge that during this period at least $2 billion of potential all-out exchange benefits were left on the table. Overall.

Specialists Economists,

Getting Bitcoin into Korea to exploit the enormous premium was unfathomably simple. The matter was getting your fiat out of the state after you sold.

Incidentally, such controls just took care of the Bitcoin cost much further, as people acknowledged Bitcoin could do what fiat proved unable: make cross outskirt installments in any sum without authorization from any administrative position.

These models outline how worldwide tumult is by and large observed as valuable to Bitcoin's cost since Bitcoin is unopinionated and sits outside the control or impact of any particulate government.

COVID19 was one such illustration of worldwide Chaos boosting Bitcoin, as the Federal Reserve broadcasted a 'plentiful stores system'.

When contemplating how financial aspects and governmental issues will influence Bitcoin's value, it's imperative to think on a worldwide scale and not just about what's going on in a solitary nation.

CHAPTER FOUR

Process To Invest In Bitcoins And Where To Buy

The problem of buying bitcoins depends on your state. Caused nations to have more different alternatives and more noticeable liquidity.

Coinbase is the world's biggest bitcoin agent and accessible in the United States, UK, Canada, Singapore, and the majority of Europe.

Step by step instructions to Secure Bitcoins

Similarly, as with anything important, programmers, cheats, and tricksters will all be after your bitcoins, so making sure about your bitcoins is essential.

In case you're not kidding about putting resources into bitcoin and see yourself purchasing a huge sum, we suggest utilizing Bitcoin wallets that were worked considering security.

Record Nano X

Record is a Bitcoin security organization that offers a wide scope of secure Bitcoin stockpiling gadgets. We at present observe the Ledger Nano X as Ledger's most secure advanced wallet.

TREZOR

TREZOR is an equipment wallet that was worked to make sure about bitcoins. It produces your Bitcoin private keys disconnected. Bitcoins should simply be kept in wallets you control.

On the off chance that you leave $5,000 worth of gold coins with a companion, your companion could without much of a stretch escape with your coins and you probably won't see them once more.

Since Bitcoin is on the web, they are considerably simpler to take and a lot harder to return and follow.

Bitcoin itself is secure, in any case, bitcoins are similarly as secure as the wallet taking care of them.

Putting resources into bitcoin is quite serious, and making sure about your venture should be your first concern.

Would It Be A Good Idea For You To Invest In Bitcoin Mining?

The Bitcoin mining industry has developed at a fast speed.

Mining, which should once be possible on the normal home PC is presently just done beneficially utilizing particular server farms and equipment (known as 'ASIC's').

These datacenters are distribution centers, loaded up with PCs worked for the sole reason for mining

Bitcoin. Today, it costs a huge number of dollars to try and begin a beneficial mining activity.

A view from inside a coordinated mining ranch

Bitcoin excavators are not, at this point a beneficial venture for new Bitcoin clients.

In the event that you need a little digger to mess with mining, pull out all the stops. However, don't regard your home mining activity as a venture or hope to get a return.

Keeping Away From Bitcoin Scams

Part of putting resources into Bitcoin is monitoring the numerous tricksters and sorts of tricks in the space. No doubt about it: you will experience these tricks.

CHAPTER FIVE

How Might I Avoid Bitcoin Scams?

While there are no rigid guidelines to dodging tricks - as the individuals who execute them are continually thinking of better approaches to cause their tasks to appear to be genuine - there are a couple of things to recall.

1. On the off chance that it appears to be unrealistic, it likely is.

In the event that a $1000 introductory venture truly could make you a tycoon inside a few years, everybody would do it. While it very well may be a conscience lift to feel that you're on top of things, almost certainly, another person has been in on it from the base and is just intending to haul the floor covering out from underneath you. In a fraudulent business model, the best way to dodge ruin is to be on the main level.

2. Be careful about forceful publicizing.

The sort of showcasing that goes inseparably with staggered promoting (MLM) is intended to cause you to feel like you're essential for something progressive. Promoters will limit the chance and misrepresent expected additions, which is rarely reasonable. There is consistently hazard engaged with contributing. Perceive that, acknowledge that, and don't allow anybody to sell you anything that is "sans hazard".

3. On the off chance that a task's fundamental selling point is "reference rewards", flee.

Reference rewards are intended to bring in sure that cash keeps on coming in, while the trick itself brings in next to zero cash. BitConnect's Price Volatility Software, on the off chance that it ever existed, was definitely not the principal type of revenue.

Reference rewards urge speculators to get companions, family, or anybody they can. While the culprits are making the most of your cash someplace on an island duty sanctuary, you're left to disclose to your closest and dearest why they lost all their cash.

What Is A Leave Trick?

A leave trick is a generally straightforward (and moderately normal) practice of slipping off with financial specialist reserves.

A fraudster may put on an ICO - Initial Coin Offering - apparently as a method for financing future development of a genuine undertaking. When accidental financial specialists have contributed enough cash, the maker of the trick vanishes with the entirety of the cash. The Securities and Exchange Commission (SEC) has cautioned speculators of the dangers of taking an interest in ICOs.

Then again, the administrators of a Dark Net Market may take off with all the assets held retained. Purchasers and merchants have a little plan of action, as they can't actually go to law implementation for help getting the tricksters.

Would I Be Able To Get My Cashback?

Sadly, it's hard to get your cashback whenever it's been lost in a trick. Sometimes the culprits are dealt with and financial specialists get some cashback, however ordinarily the main part of it is a distant memory before anybody goes to preliminary.

The Plus Token trick is a genuine model, regardless of six individuals being captured, the taken Bitcoins keep on moving, recommending that the instigator is still on the loose.

What Do I Do If I Feel I've Been Contacted By a Bitcoin Scammer?

Report them. The most ideal approach to cause to notice their trick is to report anything you think to be obscure. While it might take some time for your case to be investigated, and you can't depend on exhausted and underfunded shopper security offices to catch up, it's superior to nothing.

Furthermore, you can utilize online media to carry light to the trick, in any event to those in your organization.

Last Thoughts

It's critical to see how Bitcoin functions prior to putting away any cash.

Bitcoin is still new and it can require a long time to comprehend the genuine effect Bitcoin can have on the world.

Set aside some effort to comprehend Bitcoin, how it works, how to make sure about bitcoins, and how Bitcoin contrasts from fiat cash.

The above data ought not to be taken as venture counsel. It is for general information purposes as it were. You ought to do your own examination prior to purchasing any bitcoins.

CHAPTER SIX

FAQ

Amount does it cost to get one bitcoin?

While there is nobody cost for Bitcoin, most business sectors with fair liquidity share comparable costs

You can check the current cost in various locales. They regularly express the cost over the long haul in a graph like the one underneath:

Is It Worth Investing In Bitcoin?

This truly relies upon whether you believe Bitcoin has a future AND that it accommodates your speculation objectives. It's ideal to counsel a monetary consultant and check whether adding Bitcoin to your portfolio is beneficial for you.

We are not monetary guides. We don't offer any monetary guidance.

What is the best venture system for purchasing Bitcoin?

On the off chance that you need to put resources into Bitcoin, the best system for contributing will again rely upon your requirements and way of life. Your monetary counsel will be the best individual to converse with.

All things considered, a few people like to utilize a methodology called 'dollar cost averaging'. With this procedure, you purchase a little at once, week, or month, and so forth It's up to you to choose how as often as possible and in what amount to purchase. The significant thing is to keep the dollar sum similar to each buy. This assists with abstaining from going "all in" at an exorbitant cost. Inquire as to whether you are interested. There a tons of administrations that oblige this methodology, including Swan, and CashApp

What is the base measure of Bitcoin I can Buy?

Bitcoin speculators can hypothetically purchase 1 millionth of a Bitcoin, however, most trades have the least purchase sums they authorize themselves. You may have to spend as much as $10 or additionally relying upon the crypto trade. Purchasing modest quantities of Bitcoin will bring about higher expenses.

Are There Bitcoin Investment Plans?

The nearest thing to a bitcoin venture plan would be something like the Grayscale Bitcoin Trust, which is like a Bitcoin ETF.

In this game plan, the trust claims a pool of Bitcoins and afterward offers portions of that pool of Bitcoins to speculators. This is fundamentally the same as conventional ventures.

You can likewise select a Bitcoin or crypto IRA which permits you to utilize 401k cash to purchase

Bitcoin for your retirement. iTrust capital is our top pick for a Bitcoin IRA money market fund

www.ingramcontent.com/pod-product-compliance
Lightning Source LLC
Chambersburg PA
CBHW070501220526
45466CB00004B/1921